THE

VELOCIPEDE,

ITS PAST, ITS PRESENT & ITS FUTURE,

BY

J. F. B.

HOW TO RIDE A VELOCIPE
"Straddle a Sadd e
then
Paddle and Skedaddle

WITH 25 ILLUSTRATIONS.

LONDON.
SIMPKIN, MARSHALL & CO
1869.

Front.

FIG. 7. THE MODERN BICYCLE.

See Page 30

CONTENTS.

—o—

ILLUSTRATIONS.

————*o*————

PREFACE.

———o———

YEARS ago—before the beard which is
now white had given tokens of its approach, and before Time had wrinkled our
brow with care—we were part-owner of a velocipede. It was a machine on four wheels, fear-
fully and wonderfully made. When first we
essayed its use, we anticipated much from it,
both in comfort and speed. What our experience
in this particular machine really was, and what
was the fate of the abortion, we have noted in
our last chapter, but the recollection of it, gave
us a grim interest in the new velocipedomania of
our age.

Faith in the possible success of such a contrivance, had been for us cruelly shaken, but we are

bound to confess, that the modern bicycle, has somewhat revived it, and as an increasing interest in it, has led us to an increasing appreciation of its many merits, we have determined to present our conclusions to the public, together with such further historic and scientific information upon velocipedes in general, as may seem called for, in order to an intimate acquaintance, with all that is worth knowing of this branch of locomotive science.

It seems probable that the machine will become increasingly popular, and if constructed upon sound principles, and of good material, we see no reason why it should not deserve its popularity. As a method of comfortable progression, no machine of equal merit, has been devised in velocipedes with the modern bicycle. We do not expect any very marvellous results: we do not agree with an enthusiastic velocipedestrian out in the " States " that " walking is now on its last legs:" nor do we anticipate seeing the idea of a modern inventor realized, and railway accidents prevented by the simple device of sending " a man on a velocipede ahead of every train to give warning of any danger he may discover on the track," but it is capable of considerable speed and may be of much practical utility.

We do not of course pretend to say everything, that might be said about it, but simply to afford the intelligent reader an insight into its history, variations, and construction. No man can harness a horse unless he understands the secret of putting on the collar, and no one can manage a bicycle unless he comprehends some of the principles upon which it proceeds.

J. F. B.

LONDON, *November,* 1869.

CHAPTER I.

Introductory.

THERE does not appear to be either in sacred or profane history, any reliable account, of the appliances in use amongst the antediluvians, for the purpose of transporting themselves and their goods from place to place. In all probability, as they were a nomadic race, they packed up their tents and household gods on the backs of animals, and moved in this way from one hunting or pasture-ground to another. And yet there must have been many things amongst the possessions of that primitive people which could not be readily carried, even by the monstrous beasts with which the earth was at that time blessed, and some kind of vehicle was no doubt invented. What its character was we have no means to determine, but it is clear that there were men before the Flood who lived in considerable luxury, and who were in their way

quite as fast as men of more modern times. In
all probability they rode to their marriage feasts,
in some rude constructions of logs, innocent of
Cee springs and despised of Long Acre, yet interesting as containing the germ of the future
carriage.

Possibly the artizans of those days, as they
rolled the giants of the forest down the hill-
sides, had seen and adapted the first idea of a
wheel; indeed it is highly probable that the
artificers who helped Noah in his ark-building
understood perfectly the use of this mechanical
aid, and that their waggons and chariots were
as well wheeled as those which in later days
rolled to destruction the followers of Pharaoh
and Sisera.

If we could only find the remains of some
such vehicle, or even an axle, that had been
forged on the anvils of Tubal Cain, we should
have an interest in it, that the fossil remains
of a thousand saurians would fail to excite. Yet
such fortune is not ours, and even as we descend later adown the tide of Time, although
we continually meet with works which would
require in their construction great mechanical

skill, we still find the progress of such knowledge shrouded in darkness.

Every one remembers the story of Dædalus the Athenian, who after incurring the animosity of Minos, King of Crete, made to himself wings and flew away. Disbelieving moderns say that these wings were but the sails of ships, and they credit the clever Athenian with this invention. But whether true or false, the existence of the fable in Grecian mythology shows that the ancient mind had turned itself to consider the problem of progression, and to baffle, if possible the opposing forces of Time and space.

Mechanical inventions of other kinds increased apace, and succeeded each other with sufficient rapidity, till they held a kind of carnival at the siege of Syracuse, under the guidance of Archimedes; yet both authors and inscriptions are silent as to any machine, or conception of a machine, in any way similar to that about which we write— one that could be driven, and the motive power applied, by the man who rode it. Indeed, before the Romans supplemented their mighty skill in war, by the better arts of peace, and gridironed their empire with roads, there was, probably, no

road in the whole world along which such a
machine, if it had been invented, could have been
driven.

It is possible, indeed, although no traces of it
remain, that in some form or other the conception
of a manumotive, or (to coin a horrible word) a
pedomotive machine, has presented itself to the
mind of almost every inventive mechanic. In fact,
ever since the genius of man developed the tread
mill, the motive power, and the manner of applying it, as far as the operator was concerned,
has been tolerably clear. The principle of the
treadmill is the regnant principle in every
velocipede worked by the foot; the main difference being that in the one case the will is con-
strained, and in the other case free. And, no
doubt, also, many vehicles have been made, in
which it was possible upon ordinary roads for a
man to work himself along for a greater or less
distance. Such elementary contrivances we see
continually employed by the deformed, but they
present to the well-developed man, no virtue that
does not exist more extensively in walking. We
are told that an eminent French chemist has
discovered how to transmute silver into gold, but

the process is so expensive that the raw material is about half the price of the manufactured article, so the knowledge is useless. It is quite *possible* to sit in a wheelbarrow and to wheel yourself up a steep hill, but the position is uncomfortable, and the process involves an infinitely larger expenditure of forces than walking, therefore we never see reasonable men exercising themselves in this way.

No one, until within a comparatively recent time succeeded in devising a machine that could be driven with as little effort as was requisite in walking, and which the operator could work himself. The Dark Ages are as dark upon this subject, as the ages which preceded them and as the ages which had the benefit of more advanced civilization. There are, indeed, some Eastern travellers who tell us, that they have seen hieroglyphics on the walls of Babylon and Thebes, which represent some similar vehicle to the modern bicycle, but these rumours are not worthy of credit, and, even if true, he would be a bold man who, in the present state of philological research, would venture to say that this so-called hieroglyphic was not in fact part of some forgotten language.

We will not amuse our readers by reproducing the device here.

There can be no doubt that a velocipede is a typical thing. It represents the civilization of to-day, and it would have been as much out of place in Babylon, or in Thebes, as a hansom cab in the streets of Nineveh, or an Armstrong gun on the plains of Troy. Let us, therefore, with all due reverence, dismiss the ancients from our argument. It would certainly have been interesting to trace the gradual perfection of the various locomotive arts, and of the vehicles in use amongst different nations, but, such considerations are quite beyond the object and scope of this book, which is simply to describe one small machine.

We have now sufficiently shewn that the wise men of old were ignorant of it altogether, and having further, as we trust, satisfactorily introduced ourselves to the reader we will proceed to consider the origin, history, and present development, of the modern Velocipede.

CHAPTER II.

The Celeripede and Dandy Horse.

TOWARDS the end of the Eighteenth century there might have been seen on some of the roads near Rochelle, in France, a very curious machine worked by the foot. As far as we can ascertain, it is the earliest specimen of such a vehicle known to have existed, and may be taken as the progenitor of the modern velocipede. It appears to have carried two persons. One of them sat in front, and from underneath a canopy directed the whole affair, whilst the motive power was applied by a less favoured mortal—probably a servant—who stood behind, and pressed his feet continually against the ground, or, as some people suppose, against some kind of treadle connected with the wheels. Whichever method were the true one, the duty of this servant could have been no sinecure. The speed must have been very slow and on bad road progress almost impossible.

Even, however, on good roads the existence of
the unfortunate man who worked the vehicle
must have been most laborious. Indeed, if the
description of the machine given in the *Journal
de Paris* is a correct one, his work must have
been one to which the treadmill were a pastime.
The details are, however, somewhat meagre and
for twenty or thirty years no further steps
appear to have been taken in this branch of
mechanical enterprise. At length about the
commencement of the present century, a new
device made its appearance, and soon created
an immense sensation in the French capital.
The inventor of this machine appears to have
been a certain Mr. Niepce of Chalons, and
he greatly astonished the gay *habitués* of the
Luxembourg gardens by the speed with which
he propelled it along the well-kept walks.
The design was a simple one, consisting
merely of two wheels, one behind the other,
connected by a bar passing over them, and resting upon the axles of each. The rider seated
himself on the bar, and by pressing his feet alter-
nately against the ground succeeded in attaining
considerable speed. The machine had many

FIG. 1. THE FRENCH CELERIPEDE.

FIG. 2. THE FRENCH CELERIPEDE.

defe&s, not the least of which was the impossi-
bility of turning it. This latter difficulty, was
however, soon remedied by making the front wheel
turn upon a pivot, with a handle always under
the control of the driver. In this improved
state it came into very extensive use in France.
A representation of Mr. Niepce's machine, with
the improvement in steering, is engraved in fig. 1.
The wheels of the machine as at first constru&ed
were somewhat heavy, and, indeed, some of the
earlier imitations of Mr. NIEPCE'S vehicle were
of the clumsiest possible constru&ion. Their
beauty, moreover, was not increased by the
introdu&ion of curious devices, such as that of
carving the bar upon which the rider sat in the
shape of a horse, as in fig. 2, or in the other fan-
tastic shapes which were given to it. When the
constru&ion of the machine became lighter
and more elegant, a cushioned seat was fixed
in the centre of the bar, and after the invention
of the guiding apparatus (which the intelligent
reader will perceive to be wanting in fig. 2)
a rest was put up in front for the arms of
the operator. The height of the machine was
just sufficient to enable his feet to touch the

ground, and after it was once in motion there was then no great difficulty in keeping the balance correct if the road was good. Where there was a downward incline the driver could take five or six yards at each stride, and if the incline were a steep one he might rest his feet in front and descend without any exertion, the machine keeping erect on exactly the same principle as a hoop in swift motion retains its perpendicular.

The name originally given to Mr. NIEPCE'S invention was *Célérifère*, subsequently *Céléripede* on account, of course, of the velocity being produced by the action of the foot. But the evils attendant upon the Celeripede in all the forms in which it existed fifty years ago, were some of them of a very serious character. Many ruptures and other accidents ensued from their use, and a false step or any obstruction in the road, might give a serious sprain. Moreover, in going down hill, it was often difficult to retain control over the machine, and frequently both horse and rider came ignominiously to grief. The necessity of continually pressing the feet against the ground, besides wearing

FIG. 3. THE ENGLISH DANDY HORSE.

out a great deal of shoe leather, caused the
rider, in wet weather, to be splashed from head
to foot with mud.   And lastly, the position requisite to work it, was perhaps, on the whole
more ridiculous than any other in which people
had hitherto been willing to exhibit themselves
in public.   These evils, however, appear to have
scarcely retarded in any appreciable degree the
advance of the Celeripede in public estimation.
Its use now became no longer confined to France.
Either our innate genius, or some soldiers re-
turning from conquered Paris, introduced the
Celeripede here, and the mania for it raged quite
as hotly as it had done on the other side of the
channel.   From London it spread to the country
and young and old seem to have adopted it
with eagerness.   Its name of Celerifere or Celeripede was of course lost, and the essentially
English one of *Dandy Horse* given to it.   One
of these machines may be seen in fig. 3.

Some of the caricatures which fifty years ago
supplied the place of the comic press, were very
severe upon the new machine, and the pencils of
Rowlandson and Cruikshank, seem to have
revelled in depicting the dandy-horse rider in

ridiculous attitudes. "Sometimes we have the spectacle of a whole congregation going to Church upon the machine and leaving it at the door. Others exhibit its devotees in every absurd position that the fertile brain of the artist can invent. The accompanying caricatures copied from Cruikshanks represents 'A new Irish Jaunting Car by which you can ride at your ease and are obliged to walk in the mud at the same time.'"

Clergymen used the new machine to visit their parishioners, and to travel between scattered congregations. Postmen with their letter bags sailing in the wind, rode the dandy-horse; young swells of the period used it, not only for exercise but for the purpose of making calls; and strangest if not saddest spectacle of all, old men who had hitherto borne blameless characters for sedateness and respectability, were to be seen careering along on the dandy-horse. Sometimes the so-called horse was elegantly painted or gilt, and some apprehension appears to have prevailed that the national breed of the genuine animal would suffer from this daring competition.

It has been often said that we Englishmen take our amusements sadly, and that we are

A NEW IRISH JAUNTING CAR.

willing to work far harder for pleasure than we do for gain. Perhaps one of the most effective illustrations of these truths might have been seen when the corpulent and sober fathers of England adopted the machine.

As we have said, however, the original form had been changed. It was now constructed of the lightest possible materials, and all unnecessary encumbrances dispensed with, but still it was a strange thing for what Gray calls our "grave forefathers" to disport themselves upon. The speed attained of course depended almost entirely upon the road and the worker. If the roads were good, and the workman efficient, eight, nine, or ten miles an hour might be traversed, and this appeared to them an almost extravagant speed. But if the road was heavy or up-hill, then progression was rendered very difficult. Indeed it appears to have been necessary for the rider to dismount and carry or drag his carriage whenever a serious incline was met with. Perhaps if the incline were a short one and not too steep, it might be surmounted by increasing speed before coming to it, but as a rule the rider was compelled to dismount, or else, like the stone of Sisyphus, before the carriage got to the top it began to roll down again, and would of course frequently capsize both horse and rider. Where the roads were dirty or bad, the result was still worse. Every one remembers the happy answer of George Stephenson to the sapient lord, who apparently thought he had raised an insuperable obstacle to Stephenson's projects by asking, "What would happen to the steam-horse if a cow were in the way." "So much the worse for the *coo*." But a much less obstacle than a "*coo*" would of course have stopped the dandy-horse. Where they were driven along smooth paths and roads, a considerable amount of healthy exercise might be got out of them; and if a man had no fear of sprains or ruptures before his eyes; if he had unlimited credit with his tailor; and if he did not object to use as much shoe-leather, as would suffice for the most extensive family, no doubt he could enjoy the dandy-horse, but the numerous evils attendant upon its use, and the comparatively small increase of speed which resulted from the increased expenditure of power, no doubt accelerated its downfall, and now the

machine of our forefathers is entirely unknown,
except in the page of the caricaturist. The
cause of the disuse of the machine in France
was somewhat remarkable. It appears that an
official in the Post-office, named Dreuze, was so
enamoured of it that he succeeded in persuading
the authorities to mount their rural police upon
it, and in the summer and winter of 1830 the
letter-carriers of France performed their duties
riding on the Celeripede. One of the subsequent
winters was, however, a very severe one, and a
heavy fall of snow so encumbered the roads that
even the stoutest of the Post-office officials were
unable to force the machine through it. The
snow afterwards melted, and when the roads
presented a frozen surface it was found that the
wheels would not bite upon the ice, and that
the foothold of the driver was very insecure.
The delivery of letters became most precarious,
and the casualties appear to have been so
numerous that it seemed not unlikely that the
Post-office must establish a hospital in every
department unless the celeripede was aban-
doned. It cannot, therefore, be wondered at,
that when the next summer's sun had hardened

the roads, the celeripede was found to have lost its popularity, and was consigned to the same limbo wherein rest the alchemists' efforts after the philosopher's stone, and the thousand devices of perpetual motion.   Thus, we see that in France, Nature herself gave the *coup de grâce* to what some might consider an outrage on her prescriptive rights.   Whether the recent invention will come to an equally ignominious conclusion, time alone can tell.   Nothing but a great improvement in the system of working, could have led to the present revival of public interest in a machine of this kind.   After a glance at its intermediate history, we shall, in a subsequent chapter, treat of the Bicycle or Velocipede in its improved form.

CHAPTER III.

The Four-wheeled Velocipede.

AFTER the Celeripede and the Dandy Horse had lost their popularity as we have already noted, public interest in manu-motive and pedo-motive machines seemed to flag, and except the occasional productions of some ambitious mechanic, velocipedes were very rarely to be met with.

The Crank Axle whereby a rotatory and perpendicular motion can be combined, is—strange to say—an invention of the present century, and very soon after its first introduction several attempts were made to utilize it in the production of pedo-motive machines. The form of construction which came into most general favour was that of a frame work and seat fixed upon four wheels, the first two of which were used for guiding the machine, and the hinder two, or driving wheels, having a

C

cranked axle driven by treadles, placed upon
levers working into the front part of the framework. The treadles were placed directly under
the driver, and by the alternate pressure of his
feet downwards the axle was driven round. In
front of the machine the driver grasped a handle
which controlled the guiding wheels, and enabled
him to turn it with great facility. Some of the
contrivances were however much more compli-
cated, and allowed the hand as well as the foot to
be employed in the working. In others of
them the hands alone were brought into requi-
sition, and many were arranged to carry two or
more persons.

The sketch in fig. 4 shews a four-wheeled
velocipede worked by two operators, sitting back
to back, and using both hands and feet, or hands
only as may be most convenient.

Since the invention of the crank axle, a number
of patents have been taken out for machines,
availing themselves of the principle, but differing
amongst themselves more or less in minor details.

Perhaps the perfection of the crank-axled
velocipede may be found in one patented some
four or five years ago and known as the

FIG. 4. THE FOUR-WHEELED VELOCIPEDE,

FIG. 5. THE "RANTOONE."

" Rantoone." It combines most of the excel-
lencies of these machines, and the friction is
lessened by having only one driving wheel, instead of two. It may be worked by the hands
and feet together, or by either separately, and
by merely turning the handle in the drivers right
hand, the control over the machine is perfect.

The Rantoone calls into play so many
muscles of the body, and the speed attained by
it is—considering the great friction necessarily
attending it—so considerable, that perhaps we
can scarcely look for much further advance in
crank-axled velocipedes. A sketch of the machine is presented in fig. 5.

The expenditure of power in driving crank-
axled velocipedes is of course very great, yet as
it is distributed amongst many muscles, a considerable speed—say eight or ten miles an hour—
may be sustained on a hard road for a considerable length of time. In working down-hill it is
often found that the exceedingly rapid motion
of the levers is very exhausting, and the work
required to ascend a hill of steep gradient is also
very severe. Yet some of these velocipedes have
been in use in Wales, and amongst the hills in

Northern India, and their capacities are very highly spoken of. .

As in every other kind of velocipede a great deal depends upon the road. Where it is paved, or hard and level, locomotion is comparatively easy, but when covered with loose granite or in streets paved like the streets of some of our Northern towns with round boulders, progress is almost impossible. We have seen two men mounted on a lightly-built four-wheeled velocipede descend a hill so paved, and we have seldom seen mortals deserving of greater commiseration.

It was probably in a four-wheeled velocipede that Faraday was accustomed some thirty years ago, to work his way up and down the steep roads near Hampstead and Highgate. This machine appears to have been of his own construction, and was worked by levers and a crank axle in the same manner, as the rest of the four wheeled class.

Besides the crank-axled velocipede there were one or two other somewhat remarkable looking constructions, which excited a good deal of comment, and were attended with a greater or less degree of success, after the dandy horse had

FIG. 6. THE "GO-CART" in Excelsis.

ceased to excite public interest. One, and perhaps the most notable of these, was built on
much the same principle as the go-cart of our
childhood.

It possessed only two wheels, generally some
five or six feet in height. In the axle connecting these wheels was a cushioned ring inside
which the driver stood, and a small framework
on each side supported his arms when propelling
the machine. The vehicle was moved by simply
running along the ground and resting the body
between each stride upon the cushioned ring
and framework. An idea of it may be readily
gathered from the diagram annexed (fig. 6).
The whole apparatus simply amounted to an
arrangement for taking very long strides, and it
was attended with all the inconveniences in the
wearing out of shoe leather, splashing, and
fatigue of the operator which belonged to the
old celeripede. In ascending hills, it was often
the work of a galley slave to force this two
wheeler up, and woe betide the rider, if it
should start backwards and take him with it!

It is superfluous to say that this machine
never received any large share of public support;
here and there might be found men willing to

undertake the labour of .driving it, but the generality of reasoning mortals much preferred to take their exercise on foot.

We may indeed say that with the exception of one or two absurd machines of this character the whole period in velocipede history, ranging from the decline and fall of the celeripede to the rise and establishment of the bicycle, is illustrated only by machines constructed with the crank axle.

In addition to those requiring the use of the hands and feet, others were invented in which the power was applied by oscillating the body from side to side. One ingenious inventor indeed went so far as to contrive an arrangement whereby the hands should work one set of levers, the feet another, and the whole body should rock from side to side in concord. If men were jointed with steel or were even as muscular as the sons of Anak such a machine would be calculated seriously to exhaust the frame; but adapted to ordinary frail mortality it seemed a burlesque on exercise, and was in fact an instrument of torture worthy of the Inquisition, and eminently well calculated if persevered in, to reduce the strongest human organization to pulp.

CHAPTER IV.

The Modern Bicycle.

FEW of the men who have by their inventive genius, conferred great benefits on their generation, have lived to realize any personal advantage from their ideas, and even their names are often lost in obscurity. Whether an enlightened posterity will ever consider the Bicycle as one of the great wonders of the 19th century it is impossible to say, but if they do, it seems not unlikely that they will search in vain for the man who first hit upon the expedient which has made the machine so popular. Like many other ideas which effect revolutions in physical science, it is of the simplest possible character, and the only wonder is that it never occurred to any one before.

Instead of the operator pressing his feet against the ground at every step, as in the old velocipede, a pair of winches are fixed on to the

axle of the front wheel, at a sufficient distance
from the seat of the driver to enable him to work
them with comfort, and we have at once the
whole secret of the modern bicycle.

France claims the honour of the invention of
this simple device through a manufacturer of
Lyons, who is said to have first adopted it about
the year 1850. If this were so, and if the claim
of France is to be entertained, some reason
ought to be given for the fact, that ten or twelve
years elapsed before the idea was adopted to
to any extent, in the country.

America also lays claim to the invention of
the winch-axle as lying nascent in a patent
taken out in 1862 by one P. W. Mackenzie
for what he calls "The Cantering Horse."
The upper part of this machine was shaped
like a horse, but instead of propelling itself
in the ordinary equine fashion, it appears
to have moved on wheels, two before and one
behind. Each of the front legs was fixed to the
axle of the two foremost wheels, and rests were
provided for the feet of the rider, who was
mounted in the ordinary manner.

By pressing his weight upon the horse, the

cranks turning the front wheels were depressed
to their lowest level, and then, by rising again
and resting his feet on the rests provided, the
animal rose, and the wheels turned round. A
steering handle connected with the hind wheel
passed through the neck or head of the horse, and
thus the rider, by a similar motion to that
required in ordinary horsemanship, was impelled
forward. No evidence is given as to whether
or not this peculiar construction was ever seen
at work on American roads, and if so, what
the effect of the equine apparition was upon
the genuine beast ; but the patent seems now to
have been revived, and the patentee, or his as-
signee, has claimed a royalty from all American
manufacturers of the bicycle and also an in-
demnity for those already sold.

Neither the production of the Lyonese manufacturer nor of the American, appears however
to have claimed any public attention prior to
the *furore* for the modern bicycle, which set in,
in the French capital a few years ago.

It appears that in 1863 the denizens of Paris
were much astonished at the performances of a
French gentleman who appeared in the Place de

la Concord and on the Quai d'Orsay mounted on a vehicle constructed with the winch axle. He seemed to disport himself with perfect ease, and was attended by a kind of satellite on wheeled skates.

Large crowds assembled to watch the gyrations of these gentlemen, and every particular of the bicycle was eagerly inquired into. From that time the demand for the machine rapidly increased, and notwithstanding the establishment of manufactories in every considerable town in the empire, it was found impossible to keep pace with it. The vehicle soon crossed the Atlantic, and the streets of New York became as thronged as those of Paris with the new contrivance.

Figure 7 is a representation of the modern bicycle.

It will be noticed that the new machine resembles the celeripede, so far as the position of the wheels is concerned, although it differs from it in almost every other particular. The heavy wheels of the former are here superseded by light American hickory or steel, and the wooden bar is replaced by a strong steel spring, upon

which the rider is seated. The break is applied
to the hind wheel by simply turning the handle
in the operator's hand, and thus by a simple
mechanical contrivance pressing a leather pad
firmly against it.

The style of construction adopted in the
modern bicycle necessitates the employment
of the very best materials, otherwise it is
soon jerked to pieces and becomes useless;
we should, therefore, advise such of our readers
as are desirous of purchasing a bicycle, to make
sure, so far as they may, of the soundness
of its construction. A vehicle so lightly built,
and designed to carry twelve or fourteen stones
over thirty or forty miles at a stretch, often of
rough road, must be throughly well put together.

We will enumerate a few of the better known
velocipedes with the peculiarities attaching to
each, and afterwards devote a chapter or two to
the theory and management of the vehicle. The
ordinary type of modern velocipede will be seen
by referring to fig. 7; and the variations
from it are generally in mere matters of
detail, for which wise inventors are in the
habit of taking out patents, and then of exer-

.cising their ingenuity in discovering reasons why their particular inventions are the only ones that can succeed.

The spring on which the rider is seated ought to be made of the very best tempered steel, and the rest of the framework of wrought iron or brass. In some velocipedes the spring is quite straight, whilst in others, as in the diagram, a slight curve is given to it, which besides imparting a graceful appearance to the whole is perhaps conducive to general strength.

In many of the American velocipedes the handles are projected much farther back than in the English and French type, and thereby the seat of the driver is made somewhat more easy. It is asserted moreover that the American velocipede, of which we give a sketch in fig. 8, is both more durable and cheaper than the French type. It has another peculiarity in the framework being made of hydraulic tubing The bearings are all of composition or gun metal, and as each part is made to a certain gauge, it can easily be replaced when worn out. The axle is also of a peculiar construction, constituting in itself an oil box, by being made tubu-

FIG. 8. THE AMERICAN BICYCLE.

FIG. 9. TURNING THE BICYCLE.

lar, and closed at each end by a screw, on the removal of which it may be filled with grease or oil. This sort of axle is a decided improvement upon the ordinary kind which requires oiling from the outside, as impurities of various kinds are thus easily excluded.

The break in the French type of velocipede is applied as we have seen by screwing the steering apparatus round in the hand, whereby the pad is pressed against the hind wheel. Another English kind, patented by Messrs. Brown and Green, have a special arrangement whereby the break is instantly adjusted being part of the framework. This, called the Luton "instanter" break, has now come into considerable use, and at any rate has the merit of efficiency, as the machine may thereby be brought up in the space of a few yards. The method of applying the break, in the American machine, is by sitting back in the saddle, and so compressing the pad attached to it firmly, back upon the hind wheel.

Most of the modern velocipedes have a stirrup with one flat side which runs easily upon the axle, and is always kept in the right position by a weight fixed underneath. This has been since improved upon, by a triangular construction whereby one side of the stirrup, is always ready to receive the foot. It is claimed in this kind of stirrup, that the ancle joint is brought more into play, and the knee thereby relieved, as it allows of any part of the foot being used, whilst in other stirrups the shank or weakest part can alone be employed.

Several endeavours have been made by manufacturers to overcome a difficulty which exists in steering the machine, owing to the danger of having the two wheels turning in contrary directions when rounding a curve. Fig. 9 illustrates this difficulty. It is often found that even in a very slight turn the front wheel is forced against the leg (as seen in fig. 9) and the hold of the feet upon the stirrups thus rendered almost impossible.

Some makers have endeavoured to overcome this, by only allowing the front wheel a play of 40° in each direction : this being declared to be sufficient for the sharpest curve. Others have made the hind wheel the steering wheel, thereby always having the front wheel in a line and

FIG. 10. BICYCLE STEERED BY THE HIND-WHEEL.

FIG. 11. "THE PHANTOM,"

getting rid of the danger of the feet leaving the stirrups. This style of machine is shewn in fig. 10. The evil incident to the turning of the modern velocipede, is however, entirely overcome in a powerful but slight form of the machine, known as the "Phantom." The illustration fig. 11. will convey an idea of its general appearance.

From the sketch it will be seen that in the " Phantom " the carriage or backbone connecting the wheels together, instead of being an unyielding bar of iron, is formed as a kind of framework somewhat in the shape of a diamond. "This frame is made of strong steel bars and gun-metal ; in its centre is a perpendicular joint, so constructed as to hinge together the front and back halves of the carriage, and when the machine is moved upon a curve the sides of the front and back wheels are made to approach as though one of the wheels was about to be folded back upon the other. Each wheel turns upon its base as upon a pivot, and the axles of each radiate or point towards the centre of the curve or circle in which the machine is moving. The effect of this, as will be seen in fig. 11 is that, no matter how sharp the circle upon which it is

placed, the back wheel is turned in exactly the
same line of motion, and in fact passes over
exactly the same course as the front one.   The
saddle is attached to the front half of the machine,
and the rider moves with that half, and con-
sequently retains the same command of the
treadles, even upon the sharpest curve, as if the
machine was going upon a perfectly straight
course.   Every part of the rider's body is con-
stantly in exactly the same position as regards
the driving wheel, and in no case is it at all
possible for the legs to come into the slightest
contact with the rims of the wheels.   In the
event of a fall it is equally impossible for the
rider to become entangled with or locked between
the different parts of the machine in the way
depicted in the case of the ordinary Bicycle.
If the rider, in a moment of extreme danger,
relaxes his hold of the steering-handle, the worst
that can happen to him is that he will come to
the ground, and even then it will most probably
be upon one of his feet, and the machine will
roll away from under him.   Certainly if it falls
upon him it will not, and cannot, entwine itself
about his limbs."

Thus it is found that as each new difficulty presents itself in the construction of the machine, some method of overcoming it is devised, and we may fairly hope that before long the bicycle will approach as near perfection as modern mechanical science will allow.

D

CHAPTER V.

How to Manage a Bicycle.

WHEN an individual for the first time in his life sees a man spinning along the road and turning round street corners, seated on a bar of steel fixed above two wheels, one running immediately behind the other, and without any lateral support, he is apt to experience considerable surprise and astonishment. He likens the performance to that of some daring acrobat, and is in a state of constant fear lest the rider should fall sideways and break his head. And, even when he finds that this fear is practically groundless, he cannot resist the conclusion that such doubtful skill is only to be acquired by the expenditure of a great deal of time and trouble such as no mortal, except he be eccentric or a professional athlete, would care to give it. But this is not so by any means. Indeed we should be within the truth in the assertion, that anyone who can learn to ride a horse can, with much less trouble and far greater safety, make himself master of the velocipede. In the latter case he will find the temper of his steed to be perfectly equable, and when the roads are good, it will also prove gentle and easy to be entreated,—not like the former sometimes lively and skittish, and at othertimes surly and stupid.

The whole secret of riding and managing a bicycle lies in the art of preserving the equilibrium. When the operator finds his machine leaning too much on one side, his only duty is to turn the handle of the steering apparatus in such a manner as to cause the front wheel to turn to the same side. The steering wheel will then describe a part of a circle the radius of which is determined by the extent of the tendency to capsize, and by the speed at which the machine is being driven. An exactly parallel case is presented by a man carrying a basket on his head: —when he finds it falling on any side he naturally steps further in the same direction, thereby bringing himself more directly underneath it.

When this theory is thoroughly understood the after-practice requisite to a complete mastery of

the bicycle need not occupy long.   If the learner
visit a velocipede school, he will probably find himself able to manage a machine without help after
half-a-dozen lessons.   His great difficulty will be
at first to reduce the theory of balance into actual
practice.   The tendency to lean to the other side,
when he feels the machine falling over, is almost·
unconquerable, but when once overcome progress
is easy.   If the learner attends one of these numerous schools provided for his benefit, he will also
have the advantage of carefully prepared ground,
and will advance, by steady gradations, to the requisite mastery of the machine.   But many riders
will not have gymnasia for the purpose in their
vicinity, or will not care to learn from others what
they can readily acquire for themselves.   For
the benefit of these we will sketch out a method
of learning which may be adopted with a certainty
of success by anyone of ordinary strength and
perseverance.

If it be possible to obtain one, it is very
desirable to have in beginning, a small velocipede
which will admit of the feet readily touching the
ground, so that whenever the balance is lost, or
the rider is at fault, he may at once recover his

position on terra firma without the humiliation of falling. He should then choose a pavement or hard macadamized road free from any obstacles, and, if possible, with a considerable slope in it— say about one in twenty-five. And first, in order to the thorough practical comprehension of the steering apparatus, and the manner in which it works, let him take hold of the machine by the handle and walk alongside it for some 500 yards or so, and carefully note the effect of every pressure made upon the handle. As soon as this is thoroughly comprehended, he may place the vehicle at the top of the slope, and with the wheels in a perfectly straight line. He must then mount and seize firmly the steering handles. If the machine be small enough he will be able to put his feet on the ground whenever any mistake is made in the steering ; if not, he must have some able and muscular friend to hold him in an erect position. It is very undesirable to attempt to work the machine before the rider is accustomed to his seat. The descent in the road will carry the velocipede forward of itself, and the learner will find quite sufficient employment at first in guiding it so as to keep the balance correct. Let

him, however, always bear in mind the cardinal
principle that whenever the machine inclines too
much to any one side, the wheel must be turned
in that direction, and he will soon pass the next
point in his self-instruction.

Having now acquired an entire comprehension
of the working of the steering-handles, first by
walking with the machine alongside, and afterwards in the saddle, but without using the pedals,
we must now advance another stage. If an able
assistant is at hand to grasp the back of the
machine and keep it steady so much the better;
if not, the next step ought not to be taken without a perfect mastery of those which have preceded it. Place the machine once again at the
top of the slope, and, as soon as it begins to
move, let the steering handles be firmly grasped
in the hands in such a manner as to keep the whole
perfectly straight, and then gradually raise the
feet on to the pedals of the front wheels. Perhaps it is safest to have only one foot on at once
at first, the great object being to accustom the
feet to the motion of the pedals. No pressure
need be applied, as the slope in the road will
convey all necessary velocity to the machine.

FIG. 12. STARTING THE BICYCLE.

FIG. 13. GOING DOWN HILL

When the rider is thoroughly accustomed to the movement, and is able to balance himself without putting his feet on to the ground, he may abandon the slope and try his fortune on level ground, where the application of considerable pressure is requisite. If he meet with no difficulty here, he may consider himself as perfeȼt as anything, except praȼtice, will ever make him, and the sooner he takes the necessary practice, the sooner will he become thoroughly at home upon the new machine.

In starting a velocipede on a level road it is well, if the saddle be not too high, to stand astride of the machine, and then placing the front wheel in such a position that one of the pedals is slightly past its greatest height, as in the accompanying sketch fig. 12, put one foot upon it. The weight of the body applied to this pedal is generally sufficient to start it, and then the other foot may be raised on to the other pedal, which will rise naturally to meet it, and the art of mounting will be acquired. Where there is a slope in the road, or where an active friend is at hand, the difficulty of mounting may of course be much lessened. When the rider comes better to understand his machine, he will mount it by running alongside for three or four yards and vaulting into the saddle, but of course for a tyro to attempt such a method of ascent would be suicidal, and almost certain to end in discomfiture.

In almost all velocipedes, two projecting arms are placed in front for the purpose of carrying the feet when the rider is making the descent of a hill. Where the gradient is one in thirty or even one in forty, the machine will not require any active working of the pedals ; and, if the operator thoroughly understands the steering of the ma-. chine, and if his break be in good order, he will find it a very great comfort to place his feet on these rests and thus descend the hill without exertion. see fig. 13. The speed may be perfectly controlled by the use of the break ; and indeed, if necessary the machine may be brought to a standstill, but if the operator have courage and confidence he may descend a hill at the rate of twenty or twenty-five miles an hour without any labour whatever. A good velocipede may be driven over very rough roads without much damage, and even up a steep ascent, say one in ten, but the operator will generally find it best to economize his power by getting off and walking up hill. A well-built machine may be readily drawn along with one hand, and the change of position and muscular action thereby necessitated, greatly enhances the pleasure of a trip with it. On a good hard level road an average speed of not less than ten miles an hour may be safely run, and if the hills to be climbed are alternated pretty regularly by hills to descend, the same rate of speed ought to be maintained.

A bicycle has been driven over the level course at St. Cloud 2400 metres, or nearly a mile and a half in length, in four minutes fifty seconds ; and in a race at Vincennes over a level course of 3600 metres, or about two miles, the distance was accomplished in nine minutes 10 seconds. Where there is an incline, or down hill, of course much greater speed may be attained. In a test race, as to the greatest distance which could be velocipeded within the twenty-four hours, which recently came off in France, one of the competitors accomplished eighty-seven miles, and the other no less than 125. A party of nine persons recently left Rouen in the morning after breakfast and arrived in Paris in the evening in time for dinner, the distance being eighty-five miles. The same feat has been performed between London and Brighton, and a party of riders recently "worked their passage" from Liverpool to London by road in about three days.

To drive the velocipede at a moderate speed is, as may be supposed, a much easier art than to drive it very slowly, and prizes are given at all the velocipede races in America and France for the riders who go the slowest. It is of course impossible for the machine to stand perfectly upright, and the slower the speed under six miles an hour the greater tact is required in managing it.

When a thorough command of the vehicle is obtained, feats of agility may be practised by those who wish to excel in them. For purposes of general convenience, all riders ought to learn to manage the steering apparatus with one hand, but a good driver is able to control it without using the hands at all. Some riders vault on to and off the saddle when at full speed, sit on one side working only one pedal, or even travel forty or fifty yards standing head downwards in the saddle. Such feats are, however, rather for the circus than public use. It is difficult enough in ordinary street velocipeding to avoid cannoning against vehicles without running any additional risks by adopting new and dangerous attitudes. We are told by some enthusiastic manufacturers that the management of the velocipede is now a part of every liberal education, and to a certain extent it is treated as such in America and France, but the art is sufficiently delicate, and the position of the rider sufficiently absurd without being made more so absurd by any gymnastic performances. One genius is already preparing to velocipede himself across Niagara in a groove-wheeled machine, and other semi-insane mortals exhibit at once their fool-hardiness and their ambition by riding along the parapets of the Seine. It may be hoped if there be real merit in the invention, that the public will not be deterred from appreciating it, because of the acrobatic performances of these velocipedomaniacs.

CHAPTER VI.

The Tricycle.

WE have now introduced the reader to both the old and the new form of the veloci-pede. We have also explained the manner of con-struction, and have shown the special advantages which are claimed for each particular variety now in the market. Perhaps before concluding this branch of our subject, it is desirable to say a few words, upon the other varieties of manu-motive, or pedo-motive machines, that the modern *furore* after velocipedes have brought into note.

And first as to tricycles. In our observations on Four-wheeled Velocipedes, we noticed that some of them were in fact Tricycles, as they had only one guiding wheel, but we included these in a previous class, inasmuch as they made use of the crank axle alone, as the method of propulsion.

The Tricycle, according to the modern defini- ·

FIG. 14. THE TRICYCLE

FIG. 15. THE AMERICAN TRICYCLE

tion of the word, is a machine in which the winched axle is used, and where therefore the principle of working, is in fact the same as that of the ordinary bicycle. This will be at once seen on reference to the accompanying diagram, fig. 14. The first wheel is the driving wheel, and is worked in exactly the same manner as in the ordinary velocipede, whilst the two hinder wheels, carry the chief part of the weight.

The great advantage which in the eyes of many people, the tricycle possesses over the two-wheeled velocipede, is the comparative safety which it ensures from over-balancing. It is possible to sit still, and not to trouble yourself as to your equilibrium, whether your machine be at rest, or whether it is travelling along the road. The worker can therefore rest whenever he feels inclined to do so, and possesses a much freer use of his arms, than when mounted on the bicycle. Yet perhaps the safety is not quite so entire, as the inexperienced rider might be led to suppose. It is true that the constant necessity of adjusting your position, which is one of the discomforts of bicycle driving, does not exist here, but there is in its stead, great danger, and

almost certain discomfiture, to an inexperienced
rider in turning a corner. If the hind wheels are
close together, there is also some danger, in driving along a road, inclined from one side to the
other, because as both the hind wheels cannot be
kept upright, their multiplication is a source of
weakness : of course if these two wheels, are
some distance apart, this danger is in large
measure obviated.

In driving a bicycle along a frosty road, or
along a slippery or greasy street, it is often
found that a very small inclination out of the
exact perpendicular, will cause it to fall on its
side. And this is perhaps one of the greatest
dangers that can beset the city velocipedestrian.
In the tricycle as we have seen, if the street or
road be perfectly level, the danger from this cause
is reduced to a minimum.

After all the Tricycle is a very useful machine,
and it is by no means impossible that after the
present rage for speed and style has passed
away, its merits will receive still wider recog-
nition.

To the artizan or trader, or even to professiona'
men, who leave suburban houses early in the

morning, the tricycle will no doubt recommend itself, in preference to its swifter brother. It enables them, to carry considerably more luggage, and also if they think fit, they may on a wet day, avail themselves of an umbrella. Whether we shall even become accustomed to the spectacle of a man velocipeding himself to business, under his umbrella, of course time alone can tell. At any rate the tricycle will afford him the opportunity, if he chooses to avail himself of it.

To the commercial traveller or to the tourist, the tricycle will prove itself invaluable, as apart from the immense advantage of being able to carry their own luggage with them, they can stop when and where they please, without perilling their limbs by jumping off. The tourist may balance the steering handle, and rest to enjoy a fine prospect, or he may eat his bread and drink his wine, under the shade of the nearest tree, with no ghost of equilibrium to make him afraid. He may light his pipe, and watch the curling wreaths of smoke disappear, or dream away a listless afternoon, without the fear of an upset continually before his eyes.

It will be noted for the benefit of such readers,

as wish to enjoy the advantage of both the bicycle
and the tricycle, from the same machine, that in
many of the latter the hind wheels may be taken
away, and their place supplied by one wheel only.
The way in which this is done, may be readily
understood, by reference to fig. 14. If the long
axle connecting the two hind wheels, be entirely
taken away, and a short one carrying only one
wheel, be inserted between the two springs connecting the bar with the axle, we shall once
again have our old friend the bicycle.

An American inventor in order to guard in
some degree, against the dangers of a capsize,
which we have already spoken of, and in order
also, to make the whole machine more compact,
and manageable, has placed the seat of the rider
exactly over the axle of the last two wheels, and
has placed the driving wheel as far back as
possible, so that it almost touches the hind axle.

It is confidently claimed for this machine, that
the danger of upsetting is reduced to a minimum,
and that corners may be turned with greater
ease than on any other machine.

For the benefit of such of our readers as may
wish to construct for themselves, the safest and

most expeditious of the single driving wheel
tricycles, we subjoin a diagram of it, (fig. 15), and
the following description from an American
paper. "From the axle of the hind wheel rises
a bow-shaped brace, to which is bolted one end
of the reach, which consists of two parallel pieces
of wood, bolted together and embracing between
them an upright standard or pipe, terminating
in a forked brace in which the driving wheel
turns, and having directly over the wheel's rim,
where the forked braces unite, a break-shoe or
pad. The weight on the driving wheel, and part
of that of the rider are sustained by a special
spring, as seen in the woodcut, which serves
as a buffer in passing over irregularities of the
ground. The steering bar, which is a prolonga-
tion of the forked brace, passes up through
the hollow standard and is furnished with handles,
as usual, at the top. The seat or saddle is sustained by two cast-steel springs secured to the
front of the reach, by means of a cross-strap or
block and bolt, so that it is easily adjusted further
to the front, or rear as may be desired. The
upright tube may also be adjusted in the reach
so as to suit the driver."

E

Another form of American tricycle, has the hind axle so constructed that the wheels may be placed either at a considerable distance apart, or close together, at the will of the driver, so that the long process of taking out the axle is entirely dispensed with.

The tricycle has come into use largely in France, and to a less extent in America for ladies. Most of them seem however to have the treadle and crank axle. We shall speak of the adaptation of those of them that employ the winch axle, when we come hereafter to treat of velocipedes for ladies.

An English mechanic has, however, designed a form of tricycle, which as far as we can judge, is much better adapted for speed and comfort combined, than any other form of the machine.

An illustration of this vehicle may be seen in fig. 16. It will be noticed that two drivers are required, who sit behind the machine, and each of them propel one wheel. The single wheel in front, is the steering wheel, and may be guided by either one or both together.

. It is of course desirable that the drivers of this machine should be of equal strength, and should

FIG. 16. THE DOUBLE TRICYCLE

FIG. 17. THE DOUBLE ACTION TRICYCLE

accustom themselves to work to the same time, otherwise its course will be somewhat devious and uncertain. Perhaps the introduction of a crank connecting the two inner winches of the driving wheels would ensure regularity. If there is regularity in the driving, it will be seen, that the speed which may be covered, by a machine of this character is very extensive, and the seat, of the rider is even more secure, than in the ordinary tricycle.

One of the most recent constructions in tricycles, embraces both the treadle and crank and also the winch axle. It is engraved in fig. 17, and presents a very light and elegant appearance.

It is built of the best materials, and if driven by a muscular rider will attain considerable speed.

The speed of tricycles will as a rule be less than that of the two-wheeled velocipede. The tricycle with two driving wheels, may be an exception, as it requires even less force to produce a given result, than is requisite in the ordinary bicycle. The expenditure of forces, must always be greater, where three wheels have to be forced along, than where there are only two, and these two fixed in a direct line. But the numerous redeeming qualities of the three-wheeler, will always commend its use to large classes of people.

It is fitted for the old, equally with the young, and as we have seen is available for either sex. The number of people that a machine of this kind will carry, is of course, only limited by the muscular power of the driver. A heavy wife and numerous family, can scarcely expect paterfamilias to propel them all, but there is no reason why the melancholy spectacle which continually meets us in the parks, of men wheeling out some poor child in a perambulator, should not be done away with. Let the proud parent mount the offspring, he is so anxious to display, between the hind wheels of a tricycle, and he will thereby ensure his own comfort, the pleasure of the baby, and much more of the public estimation, than it is his lot to obtain when propelling a perambulator.

CHAPTER VII.

The Monocycle.

NOTHING is more remarkable than the revolution which any important discovery in science effects in the course of invention. We have already noted how entirely the invention of the crank-axle changed the construction of steam engines and other mechanical contrivances, in which it was necessary, that a vertical, should be converted into a rotatory motion.

And so with every other similarly important discovery. All the smaller inventive fry at once set themselves to find out new methods of application, and new forms of adapting the product of some master mind.

As soon as the great problem of our age has been solved, and some one has discovered the art of flying against the wind, we shall, no doubt, have the same process repeated, and the discovery will be utilized in every possible way.

If the particular matter of such an invention is patented, and thereby the discoverer obtains a theoretical monopoly in construction, small inventors will adopt the principle, taking care that it is just without the pale of the law, and thereby defraud the first finder of his just gains.

We shall, no doubt, have such a machine calculated to carry fifty or even a thousand people, and driven by steam, and we may also have the apparatus constructed for one, so that the ardent lover may set at nought the bolts and bars of an angry father, and fly to the balcony of his inamorata, or even plan an elopement from her very casement.

The invention of a flying machine would be a serious evil indeed, in many ways for the world. And yet we are continually told that we are on the threshold of it. We are periodically startled by paragraphs in the *Times* intimating the approach of some Yankee through the air, or announcing the advancing completion of an apparatus that will carry us to China in twenty-four hours.

These intimations, however, have hitherto proved gross delusions. They are to the eye of the mind, what the Jerusalem apple is to the eye of the body—outwardly beautiful to look upon and giving promise of great inner goodness, but inwardly a delusion and a snare.

Still we live in an age of progress, and we either are, or we flatter ourselves that we are, wiser than any of the men that have gone before us. We gird the world in a second of time, with the electric flash : we drive our steam carriages fifty miles within the hour ; we adopt the bicycle, yet still we pant for greater speed. Men are not content now-a-days, with the stage waggon carrying travellers, two miles an hour, nor the flying coach doing the journey from London to York, in four days ; they scout such ideas from consideration, and possibly with the great inventive faculty of the time, and the new appliances that the advancement of science has placed within our grasp, some method for overcoming the difficulties of aërostation will be devised; but until the dawn of that happy day, we fear we must content ourselves, with the carriages and locomotive means which we already possess, and bless ourselves that we are not as our ancestors were.

When the winch axle and tricycle were proved a success, the smaller inventive fry, at once set themselves to see whether the number of wheels might not be altered. We have already seen | what has been done in four-wheelers and tricycles, but it was some time before any inventor dared publicly, to advocate the one-wheeler, or mono-cycle. The great difficulty was where to place the man. We shall see how this problem is overcome.

And we may note to begin with, that only two tangible projects have hitherto been presented to the public, and they usurp the two positions, in which the afflicted mortal who is to ride, can be placed. One puts him in the middle, and the other on the top. Probably there would be only one position more undesirable, and that would be *underneath*.

The most reasonable of these unreasonable things, either is, or proposes to be, constructed somewhat as follows. First the wheel may vary in its diameter, from eight feet upwards; it is constructed much broader in the centre, than in the circumference, indeed the nave or axle may be three feet in length. From the felloe or tire

of the wheel, the spokes are projected to each
end of this axle, so as to enclose a considerable
space in the interior of the wheel, where the
rider is placed. His seat is fixed upon the axle,
but projects from it towards the tire, being
balanced by a large iron ball on the other side,
and by its distance from the axle the operator has an opportunity of working with hands
and feet, the cranks on the axle. A thick iron
tire binds the whole together.

We are not aware that any of these machines
have been hitherto seen at large, nor what
method has been hit upon for guiding them.
The inventor claims for it a very satisfactory
speed, something like thirty to forty miles an
hour, but what would become of the unfortunate
inmate in case he "collided" with a cart, or any
similar obstacle does not sufficiently appear. It is
clear that if he did not keep his head quite erect, he
would be liable to be caught by the revolving
spokes; and, if once he got it through the spokes,
he would probably be either beheaded without
a trial, or gradually reduced to pulp.

Neither has any break been devised, that we
have heard of, so that if the wheel got started

down hill, and did not meet with a railway
embankment, or anything equally formidable to
check its wild career, it would probably go on for
an unlimited distance, and carry the poor man in
its interior, along in much the same way that the
historical leg of Myneeer Von Clam carried off
—and, according to German legend, is still carrying on—its wretched owner.

The other discoverer of the one-wheel velocipede (if we did not fear the law of libel we should
invent a word for his special benefit, and call him
monocyclomaniac), proposes, as we have seen, to
place his victim on the outside. As he says he
has devoted "years of anxious thought to the
subject," we fear that we should moreover be
dealing unjustly with him if we did not allow him
an opportunity of explaining his theory. This
is his explanation, and in fig. 18 will be seen his
diagram. " In the first place it seems to me that
the great thing to be striven after is the reduction
of friction; in fact were it not for the element
of friction there can be no question about the
utility of velocipedes. Of course the parts which
introduce almost the entirety of this destructive
element of friction are the wheels; and, to a re-

FIG. 18. THE MONOCYLE

duction in the number, I am glad to see the attention of inventors much directed. None of the present inventions go far enough, and therefore I propose a velocipede with only one wheel, and that one not to exceed twelve feet in height. As will be seen by the accompanying sketch, the feet are placed upon short stilts, connected with cranks, one on either side of the nave, whilst the worker sits upon a steel spring saddle over the centre of the whole wheel. The invention appears to me to join the stilts and the very tall wheels advocated recently. The pace—taking the very moderate rate of revolutions at fifty per minute—will average something above twenty-five miles an hour."

For our part, we do not see why this inventor need be so modest. Why restrict the diameter to twelve feet, or the speed to twenty-five miles per hour? If the principle be good, why not extend its application, and let the rider have a thirty-foot wheel, and a speed of sixty miles an hour? The difference in safety cannot be great. If the natural outcome of "fourteen years of anxious thought" is to place the velocipedes-trian outside wheels of this size, we can only say that we pity both the thinker and his victim.

Of course we have never seen one of these monocycles at work, and as we have, from our youth up, been taught to look upon the human frame as designed for higher ends than being broken on a wheel, we have never increased our coachmaker's bill by ordering one (even if the responsibilities of paternity would justify such reckless personal exposure), but as some readers may be more ambitious, we thought it best in an exhaustive treatise to give them a description of the apparatus.

We may of course be wrong, but until the dawn of more light, we must coincide in the characteristic opinion of a transatlantic writer that "it would be as easy to keep upright upon such a wheel, as it is to sit on a chair balanced on two legs, upon the rather uncertain substratum of a slack rope,"

FIG. 19. THE MARINE VELOCIPEDE

FIG. 20. THE PATENT VELOCIPEDE

CHAPTER VIII.

Marine Ice and Steam Velocipedes.

THE method of applying the winched-axle system to velocipedes intended for loco-motion on water will at once occur to the intelligent reader. The accompanying diagram, fig. 19, conveys to the eye the appearance of the simplest of this class. It dates its origin from Boston in the United States, but contains nothing sufficiently novel in construction, to call for much remark here. As will be seen, it is propelled by the feet working upon winches, that turn a paddle-wheel, and it is steered by cords attached to the tiller, and arranged by passing round a pulley, so that they may come up, ready to the hand of the driver.

Another variety of marine velocipedes may be seen in the Bois de Boulogne. They are gene-rally made by placing a paddle-wheel between two canoes that are lashed together, and the operator bestrides the paddle box, and drives the apparatus, in a manner equally graceful with that seen in the last diagram.

In the diagram, fig. 20, will be seen a somewhat different construction of marine velocipede, for which a patent has been taken out in this country by a certain Mr. Thierry. The mechanism is worked by spring treadles, which move back each time the feet are raised. These treadles are connected with ratched wheels, whereby a swift rotatory motion is attained, which is then communicated to the paddles or the screw as the case may be.

The number of workers that may be employed on the machine is, in the opinion of the patentee, perfectly unlimited. It is also claimed for it, that it may be of considerable use in the navy in the laying of torpedoes and other similar work.

We have been, moreover, expecting a Frenchman to redeem his promise, and navigate one of them across the English Channel at an early period, but hitherto, either from the roughness of the weather, or the failure of his own courage, he does not appear to have made the attempt.

The Ice Velocipede is, as might be anticipated, an American idea. How far it is likely to have a fair trial here, it is difficult to say. The comparative mildness of English winters, and the small expanse of ice which even a severe winter renders available for such a machine, will cause its use to be very limited. In the United States and Canada the physical conditions of the earth are different, and for several months of the year thick coats of ice cover the lakes and streams.

Where the ice is several inches thick this machine proves very effective, but if it is thin the danger of breaking the ice with the front wheel is considerable. This will be at once seen on reference to the accompanying diagram, fig. 21.

The Ice Velocipede is in fact a monocycle. Its one wheel is however rimmed with a number of sharp points, which catch hold of the ice, and prevent the danger of slipping, to which wheels on ice are always subject. The balance of the apparatus is perfect, in consequence of its possessing two large skates or sledges, affixed behind, which, whilst acting as a steadying apparatus, slip easily along the ice, and render the machine both swift and tractable.

Those who have driven this machine tell us, that the pleasure to be derived from it, is little, if at all inferior, to that which is derived from skating, and if this be so, we can only regret that our humid climate prevents our adding it to the few out-door enjoyments of the winter season.

We also subjoin an engraving of what we have called a Steam Velocipede, fig. 22. Perhaps the term is not a technically correct one, and that as soon as the element of steam enters into the machine, its velocipedic character disappears. However, we give the diagram for the benefit of the curious. It will be remarked that the cylinders and their attachments to the two driving wheels are not shewn. We are told in the description of the apparatus that they are placed vertically in front of the boiler, between it and the seat, and connect with cranks on the shaft of the driving wheels. The engraving shows the position of the boiler relatively to the other parts of the machine. "The engine is a direct action compound engine of 2 cylinders, each cylinder $2\frac{1}{2}$ inches

FIG. 21. THE ICE VELOCIPEDE

FIG. 22. THE "STEAM VELOCIPEDE

diameter, and 5 inches stroke. The steering gear consists of an endless chain over a grooved wheel on the engine shaft, and passing over a corresponding wheel fixed between the forked shaft just over the front wheel. The latter grooved wheel is a wide one, and over it passes another chain. This latter chain works round the boss of the front wheel. This arrangement gives power to the front wheel, so that in turning a corner, this wheel takes a wider sweep than the two driving wheels, which go first. In travelling on a straight road (backwards) the machine is turned to either side by turning the steering wheel to the opposite side. The boiler is a vertical one, with four tubes $1\frac{1}{2}$in. internal diameter, hanging down by the side of the fire-box. The fire-grate is cast with four holes in it to receive the bottom ends of the tubes, so as to hold them firmly. Height of boiler, 2ft. 6 in.; height of fire-box, 15in.; diameter of fire-box, 11in.; diameter of boiler, 14in. The fire-box and tubes are copper, pressure 200lbs.; but 25 lbs of steam will be equal to a velocipede propelled by the feet." Great speed is expected from this so-called velocipede; but steam carriages are of

F

course beyond the scope of our present enquiry, and we leave our readers to ascertain the new varieties of them, which have recently appeared, from the scientific works specially devoted to their consideration.

We have now enumerated nearly all the notable peculiarities of the velocipede, and the machines which the invention of the winch axle has brought into prominence. Whether that invention will mark a lasting era, in the progress of mechanical science, time alone can shew. America has already gone half-crazed over the new discovery, and it is confidently asserted that walking is now on its last legs.

One of their writers expresses the exuberance of his feelings in the following high falutin' style.

" The two-wheeled velocipede is the animal which is to supersede everything else. It costs but little to purchase, and still less to keep. It does not, like one Zedechias mentioned by an old historian, eat cart-loads of hay, with carts, horses, and drivers as a relish, just to amuse Louis le Debonnaire, or any other sovereign. It does not, like Jeshurun, wax fat and kick. It is easy to handle. It never " rares up." It needs

no check-rein or halter, or any unnatural restraint.
It is light and little; let alone, it will lean
lovingly against the nearest support. It never
flies off at a tangent unless badly managed, and
under no circumstances will it shy at anything.
It is not ludibrious, like the young mule, nor
does it; like the Morgan colt, cut up in a
ridiculously corybantic manner, nor does it in
other ways disgrace the memory of its inventor.
In its movements it is all grace. Its one gait is
so uniform and easy, and beautiful to look at,
simple to analyze, that it would be a shame to
speak of a trot in the same breath. When its
driver driveth furiously, even as did Jehu, the
son of Nimshi, then there may be danger to him
who obstructs the way, and will not make room
for the flying steed. But otherwise not. When
we have nationalized the stranger, do not let us
forget his origin, but where many smooth roads
meet, erect to the memory, and in honor of the
inventor a brave monument like that which sur-
mounts the grave of him who first gave us
pickles, and taught the world how to cure and
barrel the bony herring. Let it not be said
that the maker of the first bicycle went unre-

warded by the descendants of that posterity who
forgot Ctesibius, the first organ builder, or him
who introduced the gridiron, nor yet those other
anonymous benefactors to whom we owe the
benefits and blessings derived from the use of
door knobs and buttons."

This kind of writing has a style of its own.
We cannot approach it, and so perhaps we had
better end our chapter.

CHAPTER IX.

Ladies' Velocipedes.

THE great objection to which velocipedes and velocipedestrination have hitherto been open, is their exclusiveness. The pleasures of the new mode of locomotion were confined exclusively to the sterner sex; and the fairer and frailer portion of creation, were bound to stand quietly by, whilst husbands and lovers revelled in the new sensation.

To the ladies of Paris—accustomed to the gratification of every passing whim—this was sufficiently provoking, and they have overcome the difficulty, as we shall hereafter see, by the adoption of a modified form of tricycle. But the American lady could not rest content with any such feeble substitute. She felt that her independence was to some degree at stake.

American ladies had already familiarized to themselves every other method of locomotion;

they were as much at home on the horse as their brothers and husbands, and they declared the invention of the age to be both a delusion and a sham if it did not shew them the way to become equally so on the bicycle. The ancient methods of progression they contemptuously dismissed. Time was, when the fathers and mothers of the land used to take their journeys abroad mounted on the same horse, the wife sitting behind on what was known as a "pillion." But those were the days of wifely obedience, and the journeys were pleasant to all concerned—saving, perhaps, the horse. If the road were long, and the riders heavy, *its* sufferings must have been considerable.

And moreover this position had its recommendations from an æsthetical point of view; if the road were hilly and rough, it often became necessary for the wife, in order to keep the balance, to lean lovingly against, or even to half embrace, her husband, and thus unconsciously her sense of dependence was strengthened. We have often thought that our modern style of locomotion presents nothing so interesting as was this patriarchal method of travel.

FIG. 23. THE AMERICAN LADIES BICYCLE

FIG. 24 THE PARISIAN LADIES VELOCIPEDE.

Before we pass on to see what has been done for the strong-minded and independent lady, we may perhaps note that the velocipede promises, to a certain extent, to reintroduce the "pillion" style of riding. The belles and beaux of some American cities, have foreshadowed the happy day in a vehicle which we engrave in fig. 23. We are told that this velocipede is not seldom to be seen in the streets of New York and Boston, and we feel confident that when the first blush of novelty has passed away, English ladies will be as eager to try it as their American sisters.

The device consists simply of an ordinary double seated bicycle, driven in front by the husband or "cousin," or lover, as the case may be, and with the lady, seated side-saddle fashion, behind, and working one of the hind wheel winches. We forbear to bore our readers with enumerating the advantages which may result to the youth of the land from the extensive adoption of such a machine ; they will occur to the mind of every rightly constituted male. If it be a plea-sure to take an evening stroll, or a pull on the river with the fair lady of your choice, what must be the ecstasy attendant upon planting her

on your own bicycle, and, whilst practically
driving her in any direction you incline, to still
give her a certain power over the machine?
What better commentary could be written of
wedded life than that which two such velocipedestrians naturally work out for themselves? The
man in front guides and directs the whole, doing
the main part of the hard labour, whilst the lady
behind, follows wherever he may lead, accustoms
herself to his direction, and yet feels that she has
an interest in the machine, and that its safety, to
a greater or less extent, depends upon her care
and exertion.

But, as we have said, American ladies are
many of them so strong minded and independent,
that they will have none of this. They do not
believe in looking for guidance and support to
the other "vessel." They have fought for equality
on the platform and the pulpit; in the sick room
and at the bar, and they are not intending to
allow the velocipede to remain a standing token
of the "subjection of women." This is what an
American paper specially devoted to the velocipede interest, says of ladies on the bicycle :—
"It had been a matter of doubt whether the

ladies would take to the velocipede or not, as
many had supposed that the use of the bicycle
was of course out of the question unless each
fair rider followed Jessica's example, and obscured
herself in the lovely garnish of a boy. But while
the young men, and some that, alas! are young
no longer, are dashing about on velocipedes,
the active young women look on with envy and
emulation. They do not see why they should be
denied the exercise and amusement which the
bicycle so abundantly furnishes. Many tricycles
have been designed for their especial use, but
with those they are not satisfied, and this style of
machine will not come into general use. The
ladies want a little of the risk and dash which
attends the riding of the two-wheeled velocipede,
and will hardly be content with a machine that
cannot possibly upset or run into somebody.
The idea is sometimes conceived, from seeing
experts ride side-saddle fashion and drive the
machine with one foot, that ladies might begin
by learning that mode of velocipeditation, but it is
a mistake. It would be well-nigh impossible
to acquire the art in that way, though it is easy
enough after one has learned. What is needed

is a two-wheeled velocipede properly adapted to
the use of ladies, and there is now one in use.
The reach or frame, instead of forming a nearly
straight line from the front swivel to the hind
axle, follows the curve of the wheel until it
reaches a line nearly as low as the hind axle;
when it runs horizontally to that point of the
hind wheel. The two wheels being separated
three or four inches, allow of an upright rod
being secured to the frame ; around this is a
spiral spring, upon which a comfortable cane-
seated willow-backed chair is placed. This
machine, with a moderate sized wheel (say thirty
to thirty-three inches), will permit a lady to drive
with a great deal of comfort and all the advantages of the two-wheel veloce, without its objec-
tionable features. For, instance, in mounting, a
lady would have to step over the reach at a point
only twelve inches from the floor—the height of
an ordinary step in a flight of stairs. And, now,
as to the dress. What is wanted in this respect
is a dress that shall be suitable for either riding
or walking. This, we think, has also been achieved,
and that by a lady. Let us try to describe the
dress of a *velocipedestrienne.* Let the outer skirt

be made so as to button its entire length in front
—the back part should be made to button from
the bottom to a point about three-eighths of a
yard up the skirt. This arrangement does not
detraĉt at all from the appearance of an ordinary
walking costume. When the wearer wishes to
prepare for a drive she simply loosens two or three
of the lower buttons at the front and back, and,
bringing together the two ends of each side
separately, buttons them in this way around each
ankle, and, when mounted, the dress falls grace-
fully at each side of the front wheel."

We are told that a club of New York ladies
have this velocipede and costume under their
especial care, and that there is now in the city
more than one velocidrome where the fair riders
are taught the new method of equitation.

No doubt the invention will be hailed as a boon
throughout the States, and ladies who have
hitherto been sorely troubled with their husbands
velocipedestrinating propensities, will now re-
venge themselves by mounting their own bicycles.
One poor lady signing herself "Sarah Jane
Bates," writes to the Binghampton *Republican* to
say that her husband "goes out in the day-time

and rides a velocipede, and then keeps up the propelling motion with his feet all night." She says she "don't like it." We submit that she has now the remedy in her own hands ; let her buy a bicycle for herself, and having thereby learnt the "propelling motion," let her illustrate her capacity to her husband in the same way that she complains of in him, and we will stand bail for the issue. There will be peace in the Bates' household thenceforward.

The adaptation of the tricycle, which has found favour with the ladies of Paris we engrave in fig. 24. A slipper is fixed on the treadle for the accomodation of the foot, and the progression though slow is sure. There is no danger of an upset, and the fair rider is able in case of accident or impending danger, to free herself from the apparatus without difficulty. If French or English ladies are bent on velocipedestrination, this is the machine they will have to perform upon. Of course the Bloomers and the Mary Walkers of the States cannot rest content with such a machine, but we in Europe are still so old fashioned as to prefer propriety to sensation.

It would no doubt be mighty pleasant, to go

out velocipeding with your fair friends, each
mounted on her own bicycle, but custom and
nature revolt against it, and there can be no
doubt but that it is in the "eternal fitness of
things" that it should be so. At least half the
interest of one sex in the other, arises from their
respective dependent and protective positions.
When a lady velocipedes she destroys all this
kind of subtile interest, and thereby loosens one
of the sweetest and firmest bonds of existence.
Every velocipedestrienne ought to compelled to
wear *blue* stockings.

CHAPTER X.

Velocipathy.

Possibly we have already disgusted many of readers, by the strange words which the exigencies of a new locomotive science have compelled us to introduce into this work; and to such, the heading of this chapter will come as a positive affront. It will be the last straw to break the camel's back—we beg the reader's pardon—the final limit to his patience, and we shall be heartily abused thereanent. Now therefore, let us have an explanation.

We consider that in the use of these words we have treated our readers very *leniently*; we have not even given the derivation of velocipede itself. Perhaps the wide-spread acquisition of classical knowledge has rendered it surperfluous to do so, however, to such as are fond of the romance of the study of language, we may quote the derivation of it given by an eminent American author. He says that the word "Velocipede" lays three languages under contribution for its composition. The German furnishes "viel," much; the English "hoss," well known in its meaning; and the French "pied," foot; from all of which it appears that velocipede is merely "much-hoss-afoot." We are not prepared of course to vouch for the accuracy of this derivation, but quote it for the edification of the curious.

If the reader, however, still thinks himself harshly treated in the matter of words, we may inform him that, if we had been able to discover its meaning, we should, ere this, have used a word which we are assured has become quite common across the Atlantic, viz., "Velocipedestrianisticalistinarianologist." As we expect to have some very learned readers, we commend this word to their study, and if they can make it a "household word," why so much the better.

As to "velocipathy" we consider it possesses all the elements of a good word; the syllables fit well together, and the whole has a learned and medical sound. We have most of us been sadly troubled with the conflicting claims of Hydropathy, Homœpathy, Allopathy, and other

"opathies," but in the treatment of many of the
ailments of mankind, they will have to "pale
their ineffectual fires" before the approach of
velocipathy.

This science is not burdened with a voluminous
pharmacopœia, but boasts of only one medicine.
It is a mixture of iron and steel in certain propor-
tions, and under special conditions. The size of
the dose, and the method and time of its application, will of course differ with the patient, and
strange to say—and this is a point wherein it
differs from other medical science—the propor-
tions of the mixture must always be different in
the two sexes.

We cannot pretend to discuss *physical* matters
here but we may name two or three diseases, for
which velocipathy is an infallible cure.

Where the patient is somewhat dropsical or
labouring under a superfluity of adipose matter,
we recommend an outward application for an
hour, or an hour and a half, before breakfast
every morning. The dose ought to be applied
in the open air, and, if possible, on a public road.
The cure will moreover be greatly accelerated
if the road be hilly or, better still, newly macad-

Hypochondriae and melancholic patients require a dose similar in quantity, but given three times a day until the ailment begins to disappear when it may be gradually lessened.

For atrophic, lethargic, and dyspeptic individuals this preparation is invaluable : it may be also prescribed as a sodorific.

"Velocipathy" then, is the science which treats of the effect of velocipeditation on the human frame; and let, us in a few words endeavour to ascertain what that effect is. We of course allude only to applications of the tricycle and bicycle. Men who ride monocycles are like healthy patients who persist in taking medicine : sooner or later they physic themselves to death. For some purposes of course, a monocycle is invaluable. We are told that an inventive American, places the operator in the interior of his wheel, making him drive it by turning a crank, and that with each revolution of the wheel he turns a summersault, and thus obtains considerable exercise out of the work. For confirmed cases of obesity, or for rapidly reducing jockies to their riding weight, we should think it might be useful, but we can say nothing from personal experience. G

Now, in driving a bicycle, the posture depends a good deal upon the construction of the machine. If the steering-handles are curved, and brought well back towards the seat, as in the best American patterns, the position of the rider will be upright, and the motion of the feet will closely resemble that required in walking. The grasp of the handle, with the consequent separation of the arms, and setting backwards of the shoulders and elbows, expands the chest, and gives full play to the lungs, whilst engaging the muscles of the hands and arm.

It will therefore be seen that many muscles are brought into play, and the different parts of the body fully employed. Velocipeditation has recommendations beyond those possessed by most other methods of exercise. Take equestrian exercise : you have here the most complete employment of the legs which could be devised, but the arms are often only half engaged, and the chest and lungs frequently cramped. In rowing, there is nearly as complete an employment of the body's muscular power it is true, but the votaries of this exercise are but few, and it seldom has any practical utility beyond mere exercise. Skating, swimming, and cricket are also good in the development of muscle, and for general corporal benefit, but no one of them combines the virtues of the bicycle. The veloci-pede may be used by young and old, by rich and poor, in any weather, and at any season of the year. The expense is limited to its purchase. It is a horse that will go slower with oats and hay than it will without them : riding whips and spurs are mere dead weight. Its motion is pleasant, and whilst rolling along, it is easy to maintain the graceful and indeed dignified pos-ture which so many people delight in.

The tendency of modern civilization is to ease and luxury. Men will not walk where they can ride, and their carriages are built, and hung, so as to render their motion as soft, as that of the infant's cradle. Furniture is so padded, and filled with springs, that the smallest strain on the human muscle is avoided, and as it is well-known that the tensile power, and elasticity of the frame, becomes less from non-user, we can-not be astonished that the generations of to-day are feebler than those that are past.

We hail therefore, with pleasure, this little

machine, which, wherever used, will tend to brace the nerves, and knit together the body of whoever uses it : which tends to prolong life, by energizing its physical sources, and is at the same time of practical utility to people in every rank of life.

There will be energy and perseverance called forth in acquiring the method of riding it, even although the accidents be few, and the art soon learnt. Of course it is possible to get *too much* exercise out of the machine. A certain well-known American humourist thus describes *his* experience :—

"As a horsebackist, we have been called a success. Once we rode a mile. On another occasion we rode a brindle cow home from the fair, not to add to our comfort, but to pay the aforesaid bovine for not drawing the premium. On another occasion we undertook to ride a speckled steer, but for some reason or other, his finis department had a sudden inclination to elevate itself into the air, and we dismounted over his head, simply because the mane of the beast did not amount to much for hanging on purposes. On another occasion we rode a saw-mill saw for half an hour, but we never tried it again.

" But we did try the velocipede. We got
astride of it, and started. Immediately after a
gentleman was discovered lying on the ground,
to the merriment of lookers on. Once more we
mounted the breach, if by these words a cast-
iron pad may be called, and undertook to propel
the invention. Just then a gentleman struck his
head with extreme violence against the curb-
stone. More merriment. Another attempt, and
just then a gentleman was discovered sprawling
upon the ground with his left ear full of mud.
More merriment, but not on the part of the
victim. Pretty soon we got well under way,
by the aid of two men to push and a small
boy to steer, while we were getting used to
the contrivance. But at such an hour as we
knew not of our assistants departed from us.
We made two lunges ahead, and while endeavor-
ing to turn out for a young lady, cramped the
wrong way, collided, took her on the invention
in front of us, and we both went off together, to
the damage of a 10 dollar hat and a 23 dollar
Grecian bend. The glory of that hat and that
bend departed with much quickness, never more
to return.

"Well, we tried it again. Undertook to cross the street, and accidentally ran our contrivance plump against the hind end of a charcoal wagon. We got off, while the industrious velocipede took a scoot to the left, landing in the gutter. Such a nice place to put your feet! Good deal like sitting on a grindstone turning it with your toes. Aside from the delightful sensation experienced, it strains the muscles and is more wearing upon garments. Riding a two-story Indian hog just turned loose to fat on beech nuts would be sweet cream in comparison with this invention. Sliding down hill on a hand-saw, tooth side up, would be two degrees more comfortable than experimenting on one of these contrivances— but then it is fashionable! If any of our readers have a suit of clothes they wish to spoil, seven or eight pair of legs they would lame for seven weeks, a high finished and moral back they don't care for, fifteen or sixteen yards of court plaster; a dozen or more new hats and several pairs of boots to spoil, let him buy a velocipede and commence practice at once."

By all means, however, buy a velocipede: possibly you may not require the extra legs and court plaster. If indeed the art were as dangerous as here represented; all the other "'opathies" might be requisite to quench the ills of velocipathy, but few men have such an experience. Energy and courage are requisite in every walk of life. A faint heart never, either drove a bicycle or won a fair lady, and it never will.

Finally, to every one engaged in a sedentary life; to every one who never walks when he can ride; to every one who, like a friend of ours, is never known to run save by accident; and to every one who wishes robust health, and desires to strengthen *mens sana* by putting it *in corpore sano* we confidently say :—Try Velocipathy.

CHAPTER XI.

The Future of the Bicycle.

THE progress of the Bicycle seems steady and sure. The acceptance of the machine in this country has been comparatively slow, but it seems now to be a general favourite, and great numbers of velocipedes are constructed every week.

It is of course quite clear, that if they come into very extensive use, the conditions of life must undergo a change. People have been wont either to walk, or to keep a horse, and if they become to any large extent accustomed to velocipedestrination, the world will have to adapt itself to a fresh set of circumstances.

When velocipedes become as plentiful as blackberries, or even as dog-carts, it will therefore be necessary to have some rules adopted for their regulation. In the first place, it is perfectly certain that they must be kept off the footpaths.

It would be impossible to allow the velocigymnasts to terrify peaceable people who are content to walk, let alone the possible destruction of children generally, which might ensue. In most American cities they are also excluded from the parks, and with the exception of certain selected routes, we think the prohibition ought to be extended to the London parks also. Surely a sufficient infliction is placed upon irate mortality by the introduction of the perambulator, without endangering life and limb still more, by allowing velocipeditation.

When the Dandy-horse was in the heyday of its popularity it was modestly proposed by one enthusiastic rider, that one half of the king's highway should be given up to the machine—and if the new velocipedomania were as catching here, as it is amongst our cousins across the "herring-pond," perhaps we should have the same demand again; if indeed some ambitious M.P. did not introduce a new Highway Act, to provide roads on purpose.

Already the imaginations of some velocipedestrians seem to be sufficiently ardent. One of them proposes to have a single line railroad, laid down on the side of the roads, and a groove-wheeled velocipede constructed, to drive along it. As there would of course be both an "up" and "down" line the danger of collision need not be great.

Under even existing conditions, however, there ought to be some rule established as to the respective sides to be taken by riders when they meet. We recollect, years ago, walking to a funeral—dressed of course in the habiliments of mourning—and whilst progressing at considerable speed, meeting a miller coming in an opposite direction. Both of us moved hastily first to one side and then to the other to prevent collision, but as it happened that each changed sides at the same time, we met, and as a result the funereal character of our appearance was greatly lessened. This kind of thing must be provided against in velocipeditation. If two bicycles collide when going ten miles an hour in opposite directions, the result must be very unsatisfactory —not to say dangerous. Perhaps ultimately it will become pretty widely understood that the same rule will apply here that applies to carriages of greater pretension.

But until velocipedestrination becomes very common there will be many situations in which the rider may be placed, in which he will be in considerable doubt what to do. Some of these have been tersely put by an American writer as follows :—

" If a fellow goes with his velocipede to call upon a lady, whose house has no front yard, and no back yard, and there are a lot of boys in front of it ready to pounce upon his machine, and the lady is smiling through the window, what is he to do with it ? If a fellow, riding his velocipede, meets a lady on a particularly rough bit of road, where it requires both hands to steer, is he positively required to let go with one hand to lift his hat ; and, if so, what will he do with his machine? If a fellow, riding his velocipede, overtakes a lady carrying two bundles and a parcel, what should he do with it ? If a fellow, riding his machine, meets three ladies walking abreast, opposite a particularly tall curb stone, what ought he to do with it ? If a lady meets a fellow riding his machine, and asks him to go shopping with her, what can he do with it ? If the hind wheel of a fellow's machine flings mud just above the saddle,

ought he to call on people who do not keep a
duplex mirror and a clothes-brush in the front
hall? If a fellow, riding his velocipede, en-
counters his expected father-in-law, bothering
painfully over a bit of slippery side-walk, what
shall he do with it? If people, coming suddenly
round corners, will run against a fellow's machine,
is he bound to stop and apologise, or are they?
If a fellow is invited to attend a funeral proces-
sion, ought he to ride his machine? And is it
proper to ride a velocipede to church; and, if so,
what will he do with it when he gets there?"

This writer proposes that a "mixed commis-
sion" of ladies should settle these moot points,
and no doubt if such a jury were empanelled the
American riders would be glad to abide by their
verdict. Ladies in the "States" direct affairs,
much more than they do here, and if some
American "Mill" wished to write a book on the
subjection of one sex to the other, he would probably entitle it "The Subjection of *Man*."

As may be surmised from what we have said
as to the American lady on the bicycle, their
ways are not our ways, and they can adapt
themselves to any new conditions of life much

more readily than we can. Moreover when any
new sensation arises, they seize upon it and push
it to its utmost limit. We may be perfectly sure
that the bicycle will receive every attention
at their hands. Probably the ladies will take it
under their special protection, and frame the
code of its laws. When the idea of temperance
and teetotalism first entered a Western town, we
are told that the resident young ladies ardently
embraced it. They moreover compelled all the
young men to join the Temperance Society they
had formed, and kept a standing committee
whose duty it was to see that the pledges were
not broken. This standing committee, it is
said had a very simple method of procedure.
When they met a young man member, who
seemed in a suspicious condition, or of unsteady
gait, they asked if he were willing to be tested.
The test applied was an "osculatory" one, and
if any taint of the "liquid fire" remained in the
breath of the consumer, the committee reported
him and he was punished accordingly. It has
always been a source of regret to us that in some
of these matters we English have nothing of a
similar character. When ladies take anything

under their especial care it is sure to become popular. American ladies know this, and act upon the knowledge. We should, however, have thought that the temperance society we have alluded to, would have defeated its own end, as every young gallant, would be only too eager for the test. But all this has nothing to do with velocipedes beyond perhaps shewing how thoroughly the machine will be managed if American ladies take it up, so *revenons à nos moutons.*

Clubs and "velocidromes" will no doubt be established here, as they have been in America, and the youth of the country will be trained in the use of the machine. When its professors invade our schools and colleges, it will become an essential part of a "liberal education."

The author we have quoted asks the question whether it is proper to ride a velocipede to church? We have not yet heard that Mr. Spurgeon has offered an opinion upon this momentous question, but to those who are anxious to adopt this method of Sunday progression, it may be a satisfaction to know, that the Rev. Henry Ward Beecher has already "pronounced." In a lecture given in Plymouth Church, New

York. in the course of the current year, he thus delivers himself,—" I wish to draw attention to those amusements which excite the mind, raise the animal spirits, and give free play to the muscles. One of the great questions of the day is in relation to the 'coming man' and how he is to come. *I think he is coming on a velocipede;* (laughter) a new machine that is bound to play a prominent part in the category of amusements; a toy to some, an instrument of great use to others. I have purchased two for my own boys, and there is every probability of my riding one myself. I am not too old too learn, but I hope it will not be said the velocipede is my hobby. You are none of you too old to learn, and I shall not be at all surprised to see in a short time *a thousand velocipedists wheeling their machines to Plymouth Church."*

Perhaps Mr. Beecher's prophecy may be fulfilled. As we have not that gift we shall not follow in his steps, but from the data we have laid before them, leave every one to form his own ideas, as to the "future of the Bicycle."

CHAPTER XII.

Conclusion.

A ND now let us bring our long homily to a close. We trust we have fulfilled the promise with which we set out, and given all the information which is really worth possessing as to the new machine. Historic, scientific, and speculative, we have looked at it from. every point of view, and well-nigh exhausted all that can be said upon it. We hope, however, we have not quite exhausted our readers' patience also. It must always be remembered that if it is worth while trying the machine, it is equally worth while understanding the principles on which it is driven.

Some of our readers may think we ought to have given them specific instructions as to building a. machine; but upon second thoughts we decided not to encumber the book with more technical terms. Any blacksmith and coachbuilder of ordinary intelligence can construct one from the details we have given, and the competition in the supply now renders the price very moderate.

"Josh Billings," who seems to fill the chair of peculiar humour vacated by poor Artemus Ward, thinks velocipedes are of very easy construction. He says :

"It don't take much stuff to build a filosipede. I am bold tew say that a man could make one ov'em out of a cingle old plank, and then hev enough stuff left over to splinter broken limbs, or make, perhaps, a corfin.

"A filosipede can't stand alone, and that single fact iz enuff to condemn the think in mi eye. I don't want to have anything to do with any helpless critter that can't stand alone, onless, I might addd, it is a purty woman going for to faint.

"I don't think it will ever get intew gineral use among farmers, az it haz no conveniences for a hay riggin, nor even a place to strap a trunk ; and as tew going to church on it, the family would have tew go one at a time, and the rest walk. So of course the thing is killod in that direction." H

One particular point in which a palpable de-
fect exists in the bicycle is in the great loss
which ensues when it is being driven down hill.
If by any means the wasted power could be
stored up for use on level ground or in ascending
another hill, it would be nearly perfect.

The winch-axle bicycle is undeniably the
great locomotive invention of the age. For
mortals who are sound in wind, limb, and eye-
sight, it is idle to suppose that the tricycle or
the four-wheeler can ever again come into extensive use. Its improvement upon the old
four-wheeler is immense. We remember a club
of young men in one of our northern cities purchasing—now many years ago—one of the old-
fashioned treadle, crank-axled machines, under
the idea that it would be a source of great
amusement and recreation. Perhaps so far as
amusement was concerned they were not altogether
wrong. It so happened that the streets of the city
were in those primitive days (as many of them
are still) paved with large round stones or
boulders, much resembling in shape petrified
kidneys. Now this sort of pavement is all very
well for huge broad-wheeled waggons, or lum-

bering country carts, but for delicate wheels, such as those on which this velocipede ran, they were simply excruciating. It was impossible to drive the machine on level streets, or up an incline so paved, whilst in descending a hill the shaking was of the most pronounced character, indeed almost sufficient to dislocate a man's vertebræ, or to induce interstitial absorption in his spinal cord.

When, however, by great exertion the machine had been propelled beyond the streets, its progress was still slow, and the labour required enormous. More than once the whole apparatus was upset ignominiously into a ditch, and unless our memory deceives us, one ardent driver ran over a small child. It cannot therefore be wondered at, that it soon passed into disuse, and was remembered only as a delusion and a snare : the prolific source of bruises, sore joints, and general personal discomfort.

When well-built, a bicycle ought to diffuse physical enjoyment through the whole frame, but our memory of this four-wheeled machine is a memory of something which gave most intense fatigue. Fatigue to the legs in working the

H 2

treadles: fatigue to the arms kept in an unnatural position : and fatigue to the whole body,
by being shaken as never mortal has been
shaken, since the day when Sancho Panza was
tossed in a blanket for refusing to pay his
reckoning at the inn.

In conclusion we therefore earnestly recommend our readers at once to buy, or to build a
machine. If they build it themselves they must
take especial care to use only the best tempered
steel, and the hardest seasoned wood. They must
moreover guard against any such mistake as that
which is recorded of two editors in Chicago, who
undertook to produce a velocipede on a new and
improved pattern. One was to furnish the
money and the other the inventive skill. A
large three-wheeled affair was then secretly
constructed in a cellar, but when completed it
was found to be several inches wider than the
doorway ! We are told that the editors are
still consulting whether to tear down the house
or take the velocipede to pieces.

We, men of to-day, are like the men of
Athens in the days of old, always looking out
for some new thing : it is well for us when the

new sensation has anything really valuable underneath it. We heartily embrace the veloci-pede therefore, not merely as something new, but as something from which a considerable amount of practical good is likely to ensue.

And now, in leaving the indulgent reader who has followed us thus far, we do not know that we can give him any better parting wish, than that when he has finished his course along the level roads, and up the steep hills of life, he may glide as smoothly down its incline, as when directing a descent on his own bicycle.

THE END.

LONDON:—PRINTFD BY JOSEPH FOSTER.

CPSIA information can be obtained at www.ICGtesting.com
Printed in the USA
BVOW11s0000011215

428970BV00020B/105/P

9 781165 143023